Magic Spells
of Little Tanie

Magic Spells of Little Tanie

"POETRY ELIXIR"

Khily Khilachand

PARTRIDGE

A Penguin Random House Company

To order additional copies of this book, contact
Partridge India
000 800 10062 62
orders.india@partridgepublishing.com

www.partridgepublishing.com/india

Contents

"This is Me"
Do listen to this *song* by **Skye Sweetnam**
It's one of my favorites and describes me the best

Wealth Spell

Sky, Oh! Sky
Mighty power thy

Clear as truth
No clouds of lie

Give me the wings
by which I could fly

Let me avail the whole wide world
that my wealth could buy
Jewels of all kind, bells of silver and gold
Provide me with all the treasures, my purse could hold

Pleasant Surprise

See every arise
like a pleasant surprise

That is what
nature shall advise

Catch up with time
as it in fact flies

Promises achievement,
The daily sunrise

Observing it carefully
makes us wise

Mature Morning

With our will and vigour
a position we secure

The atmosphere refreshing
its essence so pure

The morning calls
it feels so sure

It guarantees..
every weary has a cure

Sensibility pokes
a mind that's mature

Good Morning!

Creativity

Pours from sky
the gift of blue
Absorbed in creativity
the poetry so true

Engrossed in creation
enthusiasm grew

Pristine be
the product to brew

G' morn

The Good Morning Fairy

Good Morning Fairy
comes smiling

when the Sun turns up
every morning

The fairy greets
with her wishes so warm

and passes the strength
to fight hard storm

Sky of Wonders

Spread across,
fabulously it splendours

Mystically blue,
The sky of wonders

We wait for it
until it reverts

We let it go,
When my way diverts

Good Morning

Almighty

A uniting force
That which we call God

It's tied to us
Like a baby tied to mother
with an umbilical cord

While words can defeat
There isn't any use of sword!

Going On and On

Strict to us
let life warn

Best enjoyed
With a movie and popcorn

The very thing
To swear upon

That is the tale
Of going on and on

Govern

It is fate..
..once gone, it would never return

A key to destination,
The one we govern

The very heart
resting in our arms and above

Softly it speaks
The language of love

Tempting destiny
The way we do

Not only does it speak
but understands too

Story of Love

Got no match,
Spice as clove

Protecting palms
Smitten and gloves

Symbolizing passion
Bird as dove

Lives legends
A world above

That is the story
The story of love

Am Not a Thing You Forgot

I'm a tot
I'm hot

I'm everything
you're not

Killer instinct
is what I've got

Yet I like you
more than a lot

Talent is one thing
that cannot be bought

Am not a thing
you forgot

Angry Young Woman

Following is a rhyme
worth a crore

Got no idea
what future's got in store

Angry young women
isn't young and beautiful anymore

Badly missing
the smile I wore

Greeting everyone
is what I adore

It does not matter
how much I score

What matters is
not sounding a bore

Nights are for sleeping
and let nose snore

Letters drop
words pour

Papers fold,
pages tore

Extracting facts
from its ore

Like finding shells
on sea shore

Knocking softly
neighbour's door

Bringing up pets
three to four

Angry young woman frowns
when you ignore

I'm Angry Young Woman
from cover to core

Spreading magic of words
like never before

Jingles

Nobody can hurt
when you are an expert

I'm an expert
at making jingles

The point where
our personality type mingles

A Being

Attached to its roots,
the being attempts on flying

Known to the place it suits,
remains on the position it's lying

Wouldn't it know the worth of its fruits,
unless its energy keeps multiplying

Unbeatable Evolution

Blushingly it hits in,
the dawn of revolution

Brings with itself,
a multiple faced solution

No matter how much be
the cloud of pollution

The dawn shall evolve,
no one can stop its evolution

Stream

Innocently, a flower smiled to us
When we woke up from a sweet dream

Similarly, days pas us by
As life flows like a stream

We must relish it
till its extreme

Birthday Wishes

Everything goes above
The only thing that stays is love

May it be what one earns
on the day with many happy returns

Birthday wishes
From me to you

May we stay allied
The way we do

The Rising Dawn

Sprinkles affection,
the rising dawn

Showering compassion,
moves on and on

Sparkles with love
until it has us gone

Nurtures and nourishes
the rising dawn

Sparkles with love
until it has us gone

Showering compassion
moves on and on

Sprinkles affection,
the rising dawn

Glitters with nourishment,
the nurturing dawn

New Doors

Gracefully it greets,
the morning charm flows

Every new arise.
a soothing wind blows

Its calm and serenity
makes nature feel come close

Under its divine presence
thirst for life grows

We're new for the yet to come,
it understands, it knows

To our capabilities and productivity,
life itself bows

In our willingness to go forward,
our courage and enthusiasm shows

With our passion and creativity,
we open new doors

Good Morning ☺

Ajwaain Tea

Takes the form of fire,
when oxygen touches glowing splinters

Takes care of health,
when Ajwaain tea is drunk in winters

Peace and Prosperity for all

In a melodious tone,
morning poems call

Let there be peace and prosperity
for all

Life seems served on an
inclined stall

Once climbed up,
no scope to fall

Living is represented as though
in a game stall

God is fair to each one of us
whether we be big or small, short or tall

Many-a-thoughts

Amongst each of us,
lives a poet

A true treasure in us,
that no one could covet

This simple yet precious talent does not seek
a degree or to be a graduate

Yet it does depend a lot upon how the creation,
the audience evaluate

Many-a-thoughts
speaking in mind

Living their life
in forward and rewind

Some find their way
into becoming a rhyme

Some stay jumping and jumbled
as if they still have a lot of time

Time to get released,
many books to bind

Call of the Day

We wake up from a shallow sleep
on the call of the day

While dreams are still deep
in the bed we lay

Catching those dreams,
we wonder how we may

Life carries us in its streams but at several points,
attention we must pay

Dual Nature: Material and Spiritual

Although my nature may seem dual
but in it, I try and find a jewel

Jewel of capability that's individual
The duality of being of being simultaneously
material and spiritual

Solitude

Breaks the convention of solitude to be killing
The soothing comfort in lonesomeness

Solitary moments bring about, if not always, then often,
our inner most wholesomeness

Significant Difference

A property on which no one claims
Reaching the right person, is what it aims

There shall remain a significant difference
between "Gentlemen" and "Dames"

Fresh Ideas

Every end seeks a new beginning
A book that's over still holds its meaning

A finishing point starts again
though similarities are hard to attain

With original work and no plagiary,
the world fits into a small diary

Fresh ideas of today
carefree of what will occur tomorrow

Poetry is an art
which I never had to buy, steal or borrow

Carving a Path

From the cradle of dreams
towards the progressing day

The positive energy of sunrise
taking all negativity away

Carving a path for oneself
making an apt way

A flower is sweet
whether it's rose or bougainvillea

Smiled the calendula,
greeted the dahlia

Let the wild b
while pets are to tame

I know you feel the sky speak
because I feel the same

To my Sweetheart

Brightness has spread throughout the sky
You are my brightness, I'd never deny

In my life, like a sun you shine
Yes it's true, that your presence is divine

Like a sun you shine in my life
It hardly matters someone else is your wife

Greed versus Spirituality

Variety itself invites sin
Greed finds its way to garbage bin

Spirituality however does not fray
Thus expectations are swept away

Celebration

Celebrating every moment of life
Cherishing nature's playful way

Avoiding being at the point of knife,
on this very beautiful day

Memories

Many things come and go in life
but life doesn't stop

What stops are memories
Memories mustn't flop

Wild Holi

Time to mix with colors and folks
Leaving the shell of formal cloaks

Time to come out of calm soli
That is the spirit of wild holi

Happy Women's Day

Without whom
would we have swirled?

The ones who prevent
our planet go twisted and twirled

The ones who remain
kittenly curled

Women..
the ones who complete the world

Nothing is Greater than Fate

Mornings bring along with itself
the reason to celebrate

Celebrations take place
from what we create

Nothing is greater than destiny,
than fate

Natural Surroundings

The wind of ease like a calm breeze
The playful sound of honey bees

A fresh oracle is to release
With its charming charisma, natural surroundings please

One yearns to be big and strong
An ingredient that morning brings along

Million Dollar Smile

Height does not matter

Success remains unaffected
whether one be shorter or taller

Some men learn their position
when raised by their collar

Priceless be a smile,
its glee worth a million dollar

Footprints

With God's blessing
comes each morning

We make a new way,
making past a history

We commence fresh each day,
leaving our footprint behind

With God's grace,
we ever conduct our mind

Unexpected Treasures of Life

Life isn't easy
as it doesn't accept any excuse

Life is a journey,
living is a cruise

Living is challenging deal
which one can't refuse

Living is very similar
to how unexpected treasures amuse

Living is a point
where variations and creations diffuse

Joyous Heart

In the Rainbow Bridge,
I stole the colors of vibrancy

At the Love Path,
I forgot my upset moments' frequency

In the Joyous Heart
sorrows don't find vacancy

Invisible Friend

Never must we feel alone

There's a friend near us
although it may not have shown

The invisible friend always around,
towards whom...our spirituality feels grown

Poor would be our senses
if we couldn't catch his signal

The friend keeps waiting for us
His love being unconditional

Obviously Out of Sight

My mind rewinds
as I look into the box I hold tight

The box of chocolates
gifted by someone special,
someone who made my life bright

Now the special one is gone forever,
his traces felt in the twilight

I throw myself in his loving memories
when he is obviously out of sight

All a Grace

The rising sun we bow towards
Out in the sky flown have birds

While describing this beauty the
poem may run short of words
Yet it's all a grace of Good Shepherd's

Every morning a bliss so sheer
It seems like gaiety is on its duty to cheer

True love in the air
Pleasantness felt in the whole atmosphere

A priceless feeling
that nothing can compare

Magic Spell

Luck shall call you
ringing your door bell

I cast on you
a magic spell

A wonder to happen
you must not tell

You can sense danger
by its nasty smell
Therefore, you must remain protected
in your safety shell

A sprite shall stand here and there
Its flawless beauty none could compare

Don't miss a chance
to catch its message which I share!

You're requested
not to stare

You look perfect
while a smile you wear

God is never unjust
He's always fair

Test your abilities,
you must dare

A homeless pet
is worth your care

Temple be the house
in which you dwell

Destiny holds key
to both heaven and hell

Poetry mesh
in which we fell

The only way
by which we gel

May our team
build a strong cell

Magical Love

The beauty that shows on my face
is the glow of someone's love

Shine of affection
and charm of someone's magic

I wish I may deserve it all
lifelong!

Even Today

Even today.. when I recall the memories
of the way we played, the way we laughed
All my worries get almost halved

With love and affection
fate can be carved

Devotion is the seed
to a commitment that remains starved

Full Swing

Speaks so much the nature,
without saying a word

Spreads joy and positivity,
a small clattering bird

To accept our loved ones....with their flaws,
is a great thing

Thus, we begin the day with morning wishes...
in a full swing

Heart Warming Conversation with Eternity

I felt the eternity speak to me
while I was aimlessly wandering

I talked to it in return;
the conversation was heart warming

Thus it became
a very good morning

A Hand of Friendship

I keep waiting for you,
until you affirm
I stretch a hand of friendship,
till you decipher to confirm

It's reflected in your silence,
that we're still at term

You shall persist in my system,
this is a truth of which I can stay firm

A good morning, wish is conveyed,
in the birds' chirm

Surprising Letter

One morning I arise with surprise
and find a note beside my pillow

The note was from someone I barely knew
and I wondered what pulled the person below

Then I realised what would have struck
that the letter reached me the way it did

It invoked in me a feeling,
something I couldn't forbid

Team

When five people live together,
it does not mean playing manipulation

Being able to enjoy a rustic weather,
about how to handle a situation

The essence of woods and smell of leather,
relishing it all....without fluctuation

Bottom line

Love is the element
that makes life smilingly shine

May, we remember our loved ones
that's the bottom line

Potato Pie

Blue sky
dusted with pink

Throat going dry
wishes to drink

Drink the lie
of life not being at brink

Wishing to die
before I sink

Potato Pie
is all I think

Note: This is a sad romantic spell where "potato
pie" means sweetheart, who's long lost

No Matter What The Distance Be

Dear ones shall stay
close at heart
No matter what the distance be
however far

One must respect everyone
for whoever they are

Innocence is a blessing
the way it shows in a blooming flower

It takes efforts and perspiration
to reach up a desired tower

Poetry Soup

You fill my life
with joy and pride
You complete my existence
The fullness of living
you bring to me
You bring to me
in abundance

I try and return the least I could
or perhaps I could not
Thus, you find my rhymes
on your wall
Poetry soup, served hot

Look Beyond

Long live our companionhood,
long live or bond

May our friendship keep blossoming
like a lotus in a pond

Having all the characteristics
of which we like to be fond

May our courage live unfaded
never having us to despond

Loving gestures come luckily in life,
one must know how to correspond

May poems spread learning's from themselves
if only we look beyond

Obscure Destiny

It's not a pet
the one we could tame

Something we wouldn't play
because it ain't a game

Destiny is obscure
it never is the same

Sometimes obviously heavy
yet gracious like Buxom Dame

It may drawn one to darkness
or else can bring fame

It might bring glory,
or it could incur shame

Often agile
but at times it's lame

Yet it rests beautifully
within the boundary of a frame

It mostly favours
depending upon what we aim

Else it can be blown out
like a feeble little flame

Freedom from Ignorance

If one has confidence,
no one can scare
Back to the lonely corner,
as I pull a chair

I get a feeling of freedom
like inner most soul would care

Dissolved in the environment,
spread in the atmosphere

The poem is lesson of liberation,
I proudly declare

With elements of nature,
a poem I prepare

To readers of this poem,
I offer my prayer

Justice is made,
when each one gets share

A child is the kind of delight,
which no mother would spare

It becomes duty of the readers
to acknowledge the offerings if only they dare

One must realise
the fruits it bear

Candle Light

Naughty sun is...
nice and good

It keeps shinning,
the way it should

Expressions must be made
all the despite

Every morning
have to write

It's my job to express in words
as much as I can

I have to fulfil this duty
in my life span

In the darkness,
like a candle I light

As long as I live,
I have to write

Adaptations

Before putting life
under scrutiny
one must have faith
upon destiny

Avoidable is
unrequired mutiny

Adaptations can be learnt
from nature's serotiny

Merry- Go-Round

Extravagant,
as I may sound

This rhyme can leave
hearts pound

Observing nature
within and around

Every time that I foolishly frowned
I realised soon that somewhere I had drowned

Drowned as if in a well where sensibility cannot be found
And gradually I have myself astound

Astound with the fact
that I can leave my audience go spell bound

With the pleasure of a rhyme
like a merry-go-round

Lovely Moments

What a lovely moment,
the morning time

Time to think of
another rhyme

Cherishing every bit
of serenity

That is how
we reach divinity

Useless Excuse

Public throws its
critical views
Upon a talent that seeks
headline news

It attracts attention,
the things that amuse

Their influencing capacity,
one cannot refuse

Yet trying to copy them
is an abuse

And getting away with them
is simply a useless excuse

Try and Catch Opportunity

Itself offers
the eternity
The hidden chances
and opportunity

We must try and catch
which
Thus making our collection
rich

Time does not always offer
what it sometimes may

People may try to mislead
therefore one must not sway

Effort

Fortune is rare,
why run after its occurrence

Just a little bit of effort
makes a big difference

Effort to help someone in
need
Effort to construct a society
indeed

Eyes shall cry
tears of blood
Unless it finds peace,
it will remain like a flood

Sharp Sword

Poetry is deep,
difficult to encode

Their meaning is realised
when close to heavenly abode

In life time they prevent
from feeling bored

Taking out some time out to read them
one can genuinely afford

They definitely act on ignorance
like sharp sword

Hill of Success

Ignorance is heavy,
it actually has load

To us, not to fall in ignorance
a path has been showed

Towards a spiritual guide,
the devotee feels flowed

One has to work out
to keep the wisdom glowed

Barriers are many,
pitfalls are a lot

For climbing the hill of success,
life isn't that short

Believe in God

Look all around yourself,
don't you see magic everywhere

Miracle is the entire cosmos
This is a fact....to which you may not adhere

Those who don't believe in God
are all ignorant

It is him, who has created the Universe
This truth is most important

God

He is darkness
while he himself is light
He is the one
who lives in our insight

Yes, He's a magician
His creations are a miracle

He makes the dumb
And he builds the oracle

Those who do not pay him tribute
Must realise that there's a mistake in their attitude

He can do all that he wishes
from undoing an ignorant's sins
to playing mesmerising music with his flute

Untold Stories

Not many are privileged
to savour the taste of poems

Those who do.. are simply fortunate,
To uncover the proems

Proems to untold stories
that remains in mind

They are to stay there
where no one can find

Some secrets are better off
forever hidden

After all, a section of us
must be forbidden

Living

What's in a living
without ambition

Luck is nothing
but result of our preparation

Nothing comes in life
without perspiration

For everything that we sense
adds to our inspiration

Ritual

I pick up my pen
once again

To express the joys
to express the pain

Every morning
it becomes a ritual

Expressing thoughts
that are spiritual

Requirement

The whole wide world
we may desire

Yet we must ask for
only as much as we require

Only consider
if the need be dire

Worldly pleasures
we must not aspire

Justice

Fellowship matters
even though we may not notice

Sportsmanship matters
even though we may not practice

Time is the ultimate judge
even though we may not believe in its justice

Duty

Good friends are hard to find
Therefore once found, it is wise to retain

Good experience is not easy to undergo,
thus, once undergone
it is advisable to sustain

Fortune is tough to discover
hence, once discovered
it becomes our duty to maintain
Divinity is difficult to acquire
so, if acquired for a moment..
it is a must, trying to attain

Responsibility

If we stop for a while
and observe life closely

We'll find that living is nothing
but responsibility solely

Each one of us are present on the Earth
for some or the other duty

Living is an art, functioned by heart,
if only we understand its beauty

Words Pouring Out

May not be necessary
to establish a bond

Bond with each subject
that seems to be fond

Earth is a ball
moves round and round

Life once lost
is hard to be found

Words pouring out
may not always be great

Nor is it compulsory
that they be a subject with which one can relate

Early Morning

Early morning, the sky is flushed in pink
once again

The Sun has dived
in the light blue lane

The moment when
these description feels sane

Devotion is the seed of strength;
a fact to which one can't refrain

He

No matter how clever one be;
there is no substitute
to dividing lines that He has created

However smart one be,
there cannot be another Him..
..to whom we are affiliated

Happy Mother's Day

Our first inspiration
Our first teacher

Our primary idol
Our prior ideal

Our basic need

That's our mother
in whose lap, lies our world

A Beautiful Day

The Sun so sharp
The sky ever blue

Nature smiles back
Its joy so true

The head of morning
my fingertips run through

All I wish to say is
a beautiful day to you

Ever Waiting For Your Reply

Birds are naughty
Flowers are shy

Dreams are big
Ambitions are High

Thus we try
to touch the sky

Aspirations are something
None can buy

Groove to the song
"hips don't lie"

If at all you are
my kind of guy

A friendly knot
together we tie

Ever waiting
for your reply

With my wings
again I fly

Battle Won

Affectionately it comes,
the morning of retreat

Generously it makes us feel
of a journey that's complete

Life is a memo,
living, a receipt

Ideas expressed on paper
are thus concrete

I wish you a day
as bright as the Sun

A day empowered
is a battle won

Controlling Emotions

Reaction out of anxiety
is certainly avoidable

A stroke of warmth
is all the more admirable

Why should there be
a need to react

One must control emotions
and keep feelings intact

Nothing would then
ever be able to distract

Keep Trying

(160 characters: SMS size)

Ways of life
aren't easy to understand

Quizzing are both
sky and land

Mustn't we give up
and keep trying to be grand

Time slips away
like sand in hand

Hi ☺

Synonyms

(160 characters: SMS size)

It's expressed
in hymns
that anger, hatred and weakness
are synonyms

Actual strength
cannot be found in gyms

Faith continues
even after a flame dims

Hello ☺

When Environment is Depressing

(SMS size: 160 characters)

Poems are a way of expressing,
At times when environment is depressing

Wordings of poems
could be impressing

One is able to understand
to whom it's addressing

St. Valentine's

Speaks bosom
the morning of valentine

Chirps affection
my heart and thine

True love is when
two souls combine

True passion feels finer
than what we define

Love is the element
that makes us smilingly shine

May we remember our loved ones
that's the bottom line

Ardour is simple
and yet divine

Special

(160 characters: SMS size)

Only for special people,
poems I form

You are special,
your presence being warm

Often I worry
being swept off in storm

It being hard
to follow a norm

Hello!

Morning View

Ever enchanting
morning view

Charismatic as always
ceiling of blue

Mystical charm
each day feels new

Pretty like pearls
moist dew

To appeal you
With words so few

Welcome Yet Another Day

Opening avenues
to new directions

Holding keys
to love and affections

The way to welcome
yet another day

Beginning gloriously
as we may

Speaking Straight

Without talking in rounds,
let's speak straight

Exchange of ideas,
sharing is great

Without difficulty,
for dear ones, we wait

Expressing oneself
is never too late

Taking onto the stage,
solo or duet

A New Poem

As soon as I wake,
a new poem I make

I serve it fresh,
the poems I thresh

Creating a literary taste in you..
You feel engrossed in phrases, the way I do

Relying upon Nature

(SMS size: 160 characters)

Uncle Sun
plays "I spy"

Cuz white and grey clouds
have filled the sky

A simple fact,
One can't deny

Upon the nature..
we completely rely

Good Morning !!
☺

Rhymes' Genius

When you ignore me,
I feel refused

How must I approach you,
I stay confused

It hurts so bad
not to find your reply

I keep wondering
what force to apply

I'm a rhymes' genius
Who deserves you

One of us is the captain
Of the entire crew

Happy Father's Day

The ways to success,
I gradually unlock

My father, is to be credited for this,
who made me learn to walk

My ideal, my mentor, my oracle, my idol
A complete package in himself, from
Bhagwat Geeta to Holy Bible

Morning Messages Excite

Pours from sky,
the honey-like sunlight

This scene of morning,
so sweet as it might

Good morning friends,
hope you're alright

Hope as myself,
you had a nice sleep last night

From your fruity presence,
I take a bite

You may not respond,
I keep writing to you in spite

Becuz, writing to you
is ever a delight

Let us pray to God
to remove all our worries and fright

I really wish,
all my morning messages always excite

Message for Readers

Dear Readers,
Anger is the worst disease
Anger is hatred. Hatred is weakness
Animals and warriors don't hate, they defend themselves
Warriors don't kill, they punish

Karma is duty
Duty is God
Atheists may not believe in idol worship and religions,
but they do believe in performing their duty
Duty itself is a religion

Thanks for understanding
Stay blessed

About the Author

Being a school dropout teen, the author enjoys revealing her secret side, which is expressing her ideas via the observations made from the world around and beyond. "Everyone has a secret side" is the opening line of her favorite song, "This Is Me," by Skye Sweetnam.

The author uses rhymes to convey her message to people.

Printed in the United States
By Bookmasters